MOURNING:
THE HEALING JOURNEY

MOURNING: THE HEALING JOURNEY

Comfort for Those
Who Have Lost a Loved One

Rev. Kenneth J. Zanca

LIVING FLAME PRESS
LOCUST VALLEY, N.Y. 11560

Scripture quotations are from the *Jerusalem Bible*.

Appendix I, "The Custom of Death Rites: Their Origin and Significance for Those Who Mourn," was first published in *The Companion of St. Francis and St. Anthony Magazine*. Reprinted with permission.

Cover: Robert Manning

Nihil Obstat: Rev. John A. Alesandro, J.C.D., *Censor Librorum* November 26, 1979

Imprimatur: Most Rev. John R. McGann, D.D., Bishop of Rockville Centre December 11, 1979

ISBN: 0-914544-30-6

Published by: Living Flame Press/Box 74/Locust Valley, N.Y. 11560

Printed in the United States of America

**Dedicated
with love to**

the Griffins:
Mary Lou
Artie
Paul
Kathy
John

**and
with thanks to:**

Paul M.
Raol P.
Kay B.

You will have to suffer
only for a little while.

1 Peter 5:10

Contents

PREFACE:
The Generations Pass

On December 4, 1977, following an eight month illness, my mother, aged sixty-eight, died of cancer. Less than two months later my father, the same age, died of a heart attack after being "sustained" by a respirator for thirteen days.

I knew my parents would die some day. I never honestly expected them to live forever. Yet when they passed away, I was unprepared for the pain that followed. Now, after almost two years, I realize that the death of a loved one is not something that can be prepared for; it just has to be lived through with faith.

Faith informs suffering and gives hope. It does not eliminate the natural process of grief. I was as much unprepared for grieving as I was for the death of my parents. This does not have to be. We can become sensitive to the way God chooses to heal us after a loss. We can educate our minds and hearts so that we can cooperate with his grace.

Quite simply, here is the purpose of this book: to offer some assistance in understanding and dealing with the emotions that explode at this major moment in the lives of those who mourn — those who are walking, sometimes stumbling, through the healing journey.

It was the death of my parents that introduced me to the "rituals of the Lamb." Others have lost a child, a spouse, a dear friend or companion. These are all variations on the same theme. It is not *who* dies nor is it the manner of their death that is important. Rather, *it is the way their death affects us* — the survivors. The death of a loved one leaves a hole in our lives and the hurt is confusing, sad and often crippling for a time.

Ecclesiastes is sobering in its perspective on human affairs:

> A generation goes, a generation comes, yet the earth stands forever . . . Take anything of which it may be said, 'Look now, this is new.' Already, long before our time, it existed.
>
> *Qo. 1:4, 10*

Of course this is true. Loved ones have been dying since time began. But those who mourn must be lovingly patient with themselves. No matter how many others have survived the loss of parents, children, spouse or friends, each needs time to adjust, to absorb the new shape of their life. There is no short-cut through mourning.

This book is the product of my mourning and the means through which I hope to reach out to other mourners. It is written by a believer in Jesus Christ and his resurrection.

In the pages that follow, wherever I make reference to my parents, realize that they are *my* loved ones. Your loved one may be any of the relationships mentioned earlier. Again, may I remind you that mourning has little to do with what happened to them. *It has to do with what is happening to you.*

The prophet Isaiah says that God gives strength to the wearied and supports the powerless. He cares for the brokenhearted and the persecuted. My experience confirms that he does, though not magically, immediately nor obviously.

> Yahweh is good to those who trust him, to the soul that searches for him. It is good to wait in silence for Yahweh to save.
>
> *Lm. 3:25*

Kings Park, N.Y.
November 19, 1979

CHAPTER ONE:
Why It Is Difficult
to Accept the Death
of Our Parents

In the beginning, God created the heavens and the earth. When he made man, he turned the procreative process over to him. He made man a helpmate from his own flesh and said: "Be fruitful and multiply, fill the earth." Later, Genesis adds:

> This is why a man leaves his father and mother and joins himself to his wife, and they become one body.

Gn. 2:24

The more frequently experienced reality, however, is that father and mother *leave the child*. They die first.

Nature has taught us to be dependent on our parents. From the very beginning, we cannot live without them. They are like gods to us — even more real, for they are touchable and physically present:

> I hear my father; I need never fear.
> I hear my mother; I shall never be lonely, or want for love.
> When I am hungry it is they who provide for me; when I am in dismay, it is they who fill me with comfort.

When I am astonished or bewildered, it is
they who make the weak ground firm
beneath my feet: it is in them that I put
my trust.

When I am sick it is they who send for the
doctor; when I am well and happy, it is in
their eyes that I know best that I am
loved; and it is towards the shining of their
smiles that I lift up my heart and in their
laughter that I know my best delight.

I hear my father and mother and they are
my giants, my king and my queen, beside
whom there are no others so wise or
worthy or honorable or brave or beautiful
in this world.

I need never fear: nor shall I lack for
loving kindness.[1]

Could God do more? Is this not why he gave us
parents? Is this not how parents share in the
"parenthood" of God — by loving as he himself
loves? The power of our parents is so keenly felt all
our lives. When they die, the immediacy of Godlike
caring dies with them for a time. When they die, we
lose persons upon whom we have relied for our very
existence. And while it is true that an adult is no
longer a child, part of the child still lives in every
adult. The child in us fears the withdrawal of this all-
embracing affection, fears being abandoned, left
alone.

Our parents loved us unconditionally (however
imperfectly). They had to. Rarely in our lifetime are
we given *that* kind of undeserved generosity. Upon
their death, we are left without the assurance of our

[1]James Agee. *A Death in the Family,* (Bantam Ed., 1972, p. 82)

worth *just for being who we are:* their son or daughter.

People tell us: "Everybody dies. You can't be a grown-up till you leave your parents. Accept their death. God will be good to them. Trust him."

But what happens when *they* leave *our* influence?

Another man, one of his disciples, said to him, 'Sir, let me go and bury my father first.' But Jesus replied, 'Follow me, and leave the dead to bury their dead.'

Mt. 8:21

Anyone who prefers father or mother to me is not worthy of me.

Mt. 10:37

We were taught to honor our father and mother, to respect them and attend to them. Something inside us makes letting go seem unreasonable and impossible. One of our fundamental difficulties in accepting our parents' death is that we do not have the Kingdom of God as the priority in our lives. A painful demand of discipleship is that we must relegate family ties to second place. We resent this.

At such times, we realize that having faith means more than believing that God exists. It means that we must answer the call to follow without reservation.

Our parents loved us first — gave us themselves. We loved them in return. This is the way we learned to love, by being loved. Loving means sharing the deepest parts of ourselves. When our parents die, in a sense, we lose large portions of *ourselves* to eternity. They take us with them. Not an arm nor an eye, but a piece of our heart. We suffer an amputation of our emotions.

In loving our parents, we did not merely *give* them ourselves, *we became who they were*. We imitated them: their speech, manner, values. We took them into our very center. We identified with them. They took us in too. Strangely, then, *they still live in us!* We are the ones who have died. The death of our parents is so painful because it is really self-loss. When we mourn, we mourn for our self which has died. This is not selfishness. Something of great importance has been taken from us and we hurt. We are left with a devastating pain.

Another word for grief is pain. Another is loneliness. Another is fear.

Death and absence are the same experience. We feel lonely. This loneliness causes anxiety in us — a deepseated fear of being taken away from protective love. This is especially true with the loss of our mother.

We lose our mother first when we are born — wrenched from her womb. We further lose a closeness with her after we are weaned. When she dies, this is the third "loss" and it reminds us of our past insecurities.

When our parents are gone, we feel their absence. It etches itself clearly on our hearts as a reminder of their impact on our lives. The spaces they leave behind scream out to us. We notice that something of ourselves is missing. We actually feel windless or hollow. No one can fill up that cavity. We are not the same. Part of us is gone. There is an invisible leak in our being. We are oozing silent blood. No matter how old they were or we are, we are going to ache:

You, there! Call the mourning women!

Let them come!
Send for those who are best at it!
Let them come!
Let them lose no time in raising
the lament for us!
Let our eyes rain tears,
our eyelids run with weeping!

Jer. 9: 16-18

Simone Weil understood what kind of love Christ calls us to: a pure love, a disinterested love. To love purely, she said, is not to possess. In fact, it is just the opposite. It is to consent to distance; it is to adore the distance between ourselves and those whom we love.

No one is really "ours" just because we love them. They are always and ultimately God's. They are on loan to us for a time to teach us something of love. But we are called to let people be free — even our parents.

Who is this brave? Who loves this cleanly? Who has this degree of faith? Who is this strong not to lean on one stronger? Why do we put so much faith in another and not in God?

No one can come to me unless he is drawn
by the Father who sent me.

Jn. 6:44

Only God can accomplish our dependence on *him*. Like the hidden pull of the tide, he alone can draw us close. We must permit him. We do not. We balk. We cling to the shore where we can look down and see our feet. We offer a stubborn defense. It is an innate reaction, it comes naturally to us. It is called Original Sin.

Again, Simone Weil: "The instant of death is the center and object of life."[2] For ourselves, this is a formidable thought. But to think of our parents going nakedly into cosmic life can be unbearable. Why?

Simply, we have not seen the beautiful face of God. Because we habitually think of the moment of death as a *judgment* rather than a welcome. We fearfully imagine how God may greet them. We forget that God sent his Son to assure us that he who is most just is also most merciful. "I am meek and humble of heart." We forget the sensitive way he treated sinners, renouncing apostles, weak creatures and even those who nailed him to the cross.

But there is something else. We remember that we did not always love them as we think we should. We resist letting go of them until we settle the unfinished business between us. This gives rise to feelings of guilt:

> Children . . . are to learn first of all . . . to repay their debt to their parents.
>
> *1 Tim. 5:4*

How? Especially now?

Accepting the death of our parents means that we must leave undone the task of expressing gratitude, apology and affection that we *wish* we had offered when they were alive.

Actually, we *can* say these things still, but not soon after their death. In missing them, we forget that they are still alive. Death is convincing.

Impossible chore — thanking the dead. Parents cannot be thanked adequately — ever — no matter

---

[2]Simone Weil in an essay "Love" published in *The Simone Weil Reader,* George Panichas, ed. (N.Y., 1977) p. 358.

how long they lived nor how thoughtful we were to them. We are perpetually unable to say thank you for the gift of life. We are not supposed to thank them. We are in their debt, but the debt cannot be recalled nor repaid.

Just as we are always in God's debt for his goodness and only here are we most free, so too with parents. It is a lack of trust in their generosity to think that they want to be "paid back" for all they have done. Why can't we accept the fact that they loved us more than we could ever love them?

Sure they did. They were wiser, holier and more experienced in loving. They had a head start. We foolishly measure our love for our parents by the way they loved us. Why? Why should we expect ourselves to be equally mature as they? Do we think that they loved their parents any differently than we loved them?

We were programmed to move from total dependence to autonomy. Doubtlessly, in the process of our growing away from them to assume our rightful place as adults, we inflicted some pain on them. We had to — that is what it means to be an adolescent: confused, selfish, insecure. The one test a teenager is always capable of passing is trying the patience of those who love him or her the most.

Remember Jesus, at age twelve, trying his parents' patience as he set off on his own to teach in the Temple?

Isn't there such a thing as patience — waiting for things to improve, like the ability to love? Isn't there a virtue called humility that recognizes limitations? Can we not accept the beautiful mystery that God worked with our parents to love us with his love; that they were his partners in making us happy? All our parents wanted from us was to let them love us and in so doing to make their world a bit more meaningful. They had us for the same reason God made us: to love us, to share love and life with him. We had absolutely no say in the matter. We found ourselves their son or daughter. Why do we feel that we had to earn their love?

To be in our parents' debt, to recognize that they loved us very much, does not mean that we need feel guilty — only grateful.

Ah, but there is the other side too. There is the other unfinished business: anger at all the things they didn't do or didn't do well enough to suit us.

No one loves perfectly. Yet we expected our parents to. We demanded that they always be fair, understanding, patient, lenient, interested in what we were doing, sensitive to our unspoken needs, immediate with their support in times of trouble, overjoyed at our accomplishments and gentle in their criticism.

Sometimes they weren't: flagrantly, obviously, glaringly. Sometimes, their sinfulness, weakness, brokenness, immaturity, selfishness or insecurity were painfully clear to us. Affection is mingled with many other emotions such as anger and disappointment.

It is easier to remember their failings and mistakes rather than the countless ways they showered abundant kindnesses and approval on us. The hurt is more vivid. It stands out in contrast as being atypical of what we usually received from them.

Parents cannot love all their children in the same way. They have "so much" love for each. If they had more, they would offer it. Part of accepting their death is realizing this. They had limits too. In order for them to be who they were, they needed to love according to their needs. Parents give as much as they can, if this is not enough for us we will spend the rest of our lives blaming them for something that was not their fault. "You loved *her* more than me!" "I loved you the best I could." Maybe we became too dependent on them and placed unreasonable expectations on them.

It is a lesson for many to learn: people are not perfect. Only God is perfect. Some who feel cheated of parental love seek a measure of it in marriage. Here, another lesson must be learned: no husband, wife, child, friend or community can (or should) love us the way our parents did.

The death of our parents means that we are next to die. We will follow the example of our parents in this matter whether we like it or not. Destiny will seek us out and we will respond — perhaps with more courage than our progenitors; perhaps less. One thing is for certain, only faith can bring us to the moment of death — ours or a loved one's — without bitterness. Our struggle to "get over" the death of our parents amounts to no more than trying to understand their new life and ours. Resurrection is the only reason for hope.

> Unless a wheat grain falls on the ground and dies, it remains only a single grain; but if it dies, it yields a rich harvest.
>
> *Jn. 12:24-25*

CHAPTER 2
Sickness and Death —
The Powerlessness of Simon
the Cyrene and Mary

Love binds with the power of eternity. Though they remain distinct, the merging that occurs between those who love makes them larger than they were separately. This is not only true for husbands and wives, but for children and their parents.

We look into the sick bed. Our loved one shows us that they are uncomfortable and that the pain has a sharp edge. Their expressions reveal that their struggle with illness or old age has exhausted them. All that we can see are the physical effects of sickness. We know we do not have the power to wish these away. We have secured the best medical help money can buy. Still they suffer. We want to take the pain away from them, to make it easier for them. We cannot. In loving them, we suffer also, in many ways more so.

Love keeps us at their side. It holds us there, draws us into the drama but provides us with few lines. Mostly we are mute. Technology gives us the illusion that we have control over many aspects of life. Death instructs us in the limits of that control.

My father died of a heart attack. A respirator "kept him alive" for thirteen days. The machine could not repair nor restore the parts of his brain that had starved to death for lack of oxygen. Machines have perimeters too.

Another word for powerlessness is *helplessness*. Another is *poverty*. It reminds me of one who felt the same way, a man named Simon the Cyrene. We can learn from the striking parallels between him and those who watch the suffering of another.

> As they were leading him away they *seized* a man, Simon from Cyrene, who was coming in from the country, *and made him shoulder the cross* and carry it behind Jesus.
>
> *Lk. 23:26*

Simon was one of 180,000 people in Jerusalem on the day Jesus was crucified. He was a foreigner, from Libya, visiting the Holy City for Passover. He had made this journey every year since he was at least twelve. He probably walked from his home to Jerusalem. He was remarkably zealous in his desire to praise God in what he believed to be the very heart of his religion: the Jerusalem Temple.

He did not know Jesus of Nazareth. He did not know what was going on in the life of Jesus. He was on the final leg of his pilgrimage and there, ahead of him, was a crowd and a din. His curiosity brought him closer and before he realized what was happening, he was grabbed and forced to play a role in the spectacle.

Simon had no lines either.

All his plans would have to be revised. A passive part was thrust upon him: carry *another's* burden; take on a condemned man's guilt sentence; carry a dying man's cross for at least a quarter of a mile — the grueling final ascent.

And he had to walk *behind* Jesus. He could not

even determine his own pace. *His* agony increased as Jesus became weaker, slower. Simon could not drop the cross, could not refuse to stand there and wait for Jesus to pick himself up. He had no options. He was without alternatives. He did not even love Jesus. He was there for the climb to Golgotha against his will. Powerlessness.

Powerlessness. This is what we feel when we visit our dying parents whom we love. This is why we clench our fists when we see them linger and fail to respond to medication, prayer or our love. This is what breaks our heart.

Powerlessness. It summarizes the experience of watching them become immortal during their last moments on earth. It is what we feel when we take their hand in ours and dare to say: "I love you, mom," "I love you, dad" . . . . and they don't seem to hear.

Mary knew true weakness all her life: only to watch and wait in hope. She had said, "Let it be done to me according to thy word." She had no recourse except to rely on God alone for support. No human effort would make much difference and the hand of God was not always easy to detect through the tears — especially once her son began his public life.

Simon and Mary were suffering, yet it was Jesus who had to endure the nails and the crown of thorns, the nakedness and the jeering. With Simon, we say: "Of all the others in this city, *why me?*" With Mary, we wait in silence and say: "There must be more."

We sit in hospital corridors or in living rooms and we dissect every sentence of the doctor's last report. The relatives gather from the far corners of their private lives to sit with us. We retell stories of the good times, the definite accomplishments, the virtues, the legacies of wit and charm that were not equally distributed among the children. We talk in whispers as if the subject of our parents' death is, in itself, something of great holiness.

Newspapers and books are just blurs before our eyes. Food has no taste. We are always thirsty. There is nowhere else we'd rather be than here, yet being here increases the frustration. There is nothing to do but wait and pray. Time sleeps.

So we wait like Simon, like Mary. We try to figure out what to pray for. We stand over the bed, call a name, place a kiss, hold a hand, wipe a forehead. We sing. We cry and the march to Golgotha continues — we plodding behind.

For some, it is a terrible scene: tubes, machines, spastic twitches, contorted expressions, thin yellow skin through ribs which look like sad smiles, unmentionable odors, rhythmic clicks or beeps or flashes. If unconscious, there is the monotonous non-expression: the terrible not knowing if they are aware of what is going on.

What does it matter? What if they are retreating from the senses because of terrible pain and don't know, can't know that we are there, attentive, eager to play Comforter. What if all they see is darkness and hear only their own heartbeat? What if their last memory of life is that of loneliness?

For others it is so sudden: a phone call, a quick dash to the emergency room to be greeted with: ''I am sorry, but . . . '' For these, denial is sanity. Is life *that* fragile? She was so healthy, strong and alive. There is no time to get ready to let go. There is the futile wish to replay the last twenty-four hours just to say: ''We did not mean to take you for granted.''

Something is wrenched from us by a stronger, invisible power. Not even our love can bring them back. We are frightened by the awareness that our defenses against death are paltry. Death has been all around us all the time. Now we see it. It is not manageable — not by us anyway.

And then, on the way home from the hospital, there is the terrible question: "Has our reverence for God been only gratitude and no more? Have we loved God only because we have been spared the crosses? Why are we not as grateful for the suffering as we were for the joy?"

Simon must have cursed all the way to the place of execution. He had not counted on this. He might have wished he'd never come to Jerusalem. He might have wished that Jesus would *run* to his death: "Hurry! Hurry! Die and leave me to continue the business of my life that has come to a grinding halt because of you. Die and liberate me from the ordeal. Let me be on my way."

Powerlessness makes us feel ugly about ourselves. It brings up all our insecurities and vanities, all our shallowness and weakness. The longer the experience of helplessness, the nastier we get, the more impatient, angry, cynical and selfish. Powerlessness that is prolonged applies pressure to the cracks and faults in our personalities. It magnifies and distorts our imperfections. The Evil One uses it to make us turn on ourselves. Little voices, quite real, want us to acknowledge our despair and embarassment; want us to feel terrible about feeling the way we do; want to convict us. These voices clatter and will not be still. Not yet, that is. In time, they will tire and fall silent.

Thus weakened, we are very critical: the doctors

are too vague, too busy and they don't know what to say anyway; the medication is improperly prescribed and administered; the nurses are too cool and the bills will be too high!

"Why doesn't somebody tell me something definite? That is my *father* there! He is not just another comatose patient."

Outside, down the street, the sun shines somewhere. Life is going on normally. Members of families are blissfully insensitive to one another. Somewhere, everything is under control.

> Anyone who does not take his cross and follow in my footsteps is not worthy of me.
>
> *Mt. 10:38*

It sounds as if Jesus is calling us to be Simons, not saviors. I'll gladly bear *my* cross, Lord. But why is my cross *his* cross or *her* cross? Why is my cross not something that sits in the saddle of my shoulder?

Because then it would not be a cross! A cross is a cross only when you don't want it and when it makes you aware of the limits of your strength. A cross is a cross only when it is heavier and more cumbersome than you can manage. A cross is a cross only when it renders you powerless and you are forced to trust completely in God or another to help you carry it. A cross is a cross only if it is Jesus' cross. A cross is a footprint of God stamped into the very marrow of your humanity. Anything else is only a great pain or inconvenience.

> For it is when I am weak that I am strong.
>
> *2 Cor. 12:10*

> God's weakness is stronger than human strength.
>
> *1 Cor. 1:25*

Who wants *that* kind of strength? Why does the other's pain hurt me more than my own?

Because it is not the other's pain! It is yours! In loving them you have made it so! Love has welded you! Your parent is overflowing with pain. You are taking up his/her excess. In that bed is your flesh; your blood. This is your Genesis and Exodus. The space between the bed and your feet is an illusion. Networks of empathy are alive and working between you. His blood, her bones, transmit to agents in your body — living descendents of their life.

I was in the room when my mother died. I did not realize she was dead until the nurse consoled me. It is not easy to distinguish life from death in some cases. Even after death, all the cells in the body continue to breathe on their own for a while. They die individually after different lengths of time.

Pietà in reverse: the child alone with the dead parent.

Suddenly, it is completely *our* tragedy. The focus shifts. Powerlessness gives way to desperation:

> Save me, God! The water is already up to
> my neck!
> I am sinking in the deepest swamp,
> there is no foothold;
> I have stepped into deep water and the
> waves are washing over me.
>
> Ps. 69:1-3

Again, Mary. She was there, the only one from the very beginning in quiet Bethlehem to the finale in the Holy City. She saw her innocent son and his cross and her son's Simon in parade from some obscure vantage point. She suffered with him. She saw; she knew the pain of that lance through Jesus' side. It had pierced her long ago.

Mary would remember the day of death. As he passed by she hardly recognized him except for the sign that preceded him: "Jesus of Nazareth, King of the Jews." They had time to exchange one long look, their suffering eyes acknowledging the truth that is unspeakable: that God reveals mercy *even here* in degradation and apparent defeat.

Mary was no threat to the Roman state; she could not take his cross even if she were permitted to. Her voice was that of one small dove amidst a tempest of crows. Still, she was there. Her flesh. Her boy. His pain. Her pain. His heartbreak. Her sorrow.

There were no magical interruptions by hosts of archangels; no supernatural muscle making the steps easier. Just mystery and her faith: "There is something more."

Simon and Mary died in another way on Good Friday, a way more fundamental than physical. They died to the world by accepting what they never thought they wanted: "Simon — the loss of his freedom; Mary — the death of her son. But in what they thought would be the most remote territory, both found God as God chose to reveal himself on that day: as a *Lamb,* not a *Warrior.*

Simon and Mary are witnesses to what we have endured on the crucifix of our affections for those who suffer. They are models that can give us hope. The goodhearted, the brokenhearted, are never far from God. In Christianity, we must be humble enough to know that darkness is only the overture to the bringing of the light and that the mystery of salvation is a three-act drama that is never ending in its effect on our lives.

Already there is a legacy of our helplessness that

we can spend to enrich our lives and serve our brothers and sisters. If we can finally *accept* what has happened and not hold on to disappointment, we will be able to heal others who suffer what we have been through. We will be a living treasure of compassion, a fountain of mercy and understanding for others. We will be a wellspring of strength. We will have learned the great insight into what many never understand. We will have a perspective on the future. We will have been stretched. With Jeremiah, we will have the calm and wisdom that comes from knowing in our heart this secret:

> . . . the course of man is not in his control,
> nor is it in man's power as he goes his way to
> guide his steps.

Jer. 10:23

What do you think Jesus said to Simon when they met in Paradise?

CHAPTER THREE:
Mourning

I have just returned from a visit to my parents'
grave. It is two years since we put them there. A new
stone has been placed at the site and the earth has
just settled. It takes time for things to settle. Holes in
the earth or in the emotions do not quickly repair
themselves. Cutting the earth with a spade is to do
violence to it. Losing our parents, especially after
having them with us for a long time, is a kind of
violence against our hearts. No time is an easy time
to lose someone we love.

Mourning is about pain: our pain, the pain of
the *survivors*. The death of our parents is a
devastating event which will become part of our
history, eventually. Its influence will be with us for
the rest of our lives. It has already changed us, the
way we think of ourselves, our sense of time. It is not
likely that we will be our "old selves" again.

Scripture recognizes the need and value of
mourning:

> My son, shed tears over a dead man, and in-
> tone the lament to show your own deep
> grief; bury his body with due ceremonial,
> and do not neglect to honour his grave.

Weep bitterly, wail most fervently; observe the mourning the dead man deserves, one day, or two, to avoid comment, and then be comforted in your sorrow; Let grief end with the funeral!

Ecc. 38: 16-18

It would be wonderful if we could follow that time table: "Let grief end with the funeral"! *That is when it really just begins!*

During this time, reality has to set in. While our parents are gone, our habits of dealing with them and our memories of them still linger. They do not end with the funeral. This is what "adjusting" means — letting our lives catch up with death.

The other day, my sister was talking casually on the phone. I asked her if she was "speaking to mom?" Not long ago, it dawned on me that I had not heard from my dad in a while!

Because most of us are healthy, we do not wish to punish ourselves nor cause ourselves unnecessary pain. But this should not be mistaken for fear of facing what is painful. There is a danger in being afraid to mourn, afraid to think about the consequences of the ordeal we have been and are going through.

"I don't want to talk about it," or "I try to keep busy and just not think about it" are expressions of *evasion*. Other ways of denying grief: denial that the event has had any effect on us, repression of memories of the dead, fantasizing that they are still alive, apathy, exaggerated activity, intensified sexual life, use of drugs, use of alcohol or hypochondria. One can only *postpone* mourning, *never escape* it. If we fail to allow ourselves to mourn, the process will force itself upon us: our sorrow will continue to seek expression in "substitute" forms — depression, irritability, dissatisfaction with life and possibly the permanent loss of physical and mental health.

We need not defend ourselves against mourning. It is our salvation. It is the way we will be healed of our loss. Another name for mourning is "painful healing."

We are larger than our fear. Scripture provides us with several examples of other human beings who were faced with the task of mourning and who did so — each in their own way. Let us look at a few.

David. He accepted graciously the death of his first child by Bathsheba. But when his son, Absalom, died — it was another matter:

> The king shuddered. He went up to the room . . . and burst into tears, and weeping said, 'My son Absalom! My son! My son Absalom! Would I had died in your place! . . . And the day's victory was turned to mourning . . . because the king was grieving for his son . . . The king had veiled his face and was crying aloud . . . .
>
> *2 Sam. 19:1, 3, 5*

David was wild with weeping. He wished he could change places with the dead. This was a healthy response to the loss of his son. It was his way of reacting to unbearable pain.

Job. He was different. He had suffered a series of disasters: his sons and daughters were killed in an accident, lightning set his flocks ablaze, his material possessions were taken away by his enemies and his servants were put to death. Job lamented:

In the end it was Job who broke the silence and cursed the day of his birth. This is what he said: 'May the day perish when I was born, and the night that told of a boy conceived. May that day be darkness, may God on high have no thought for it, may no light shine on it.'

Jb. 3:1-4

Job's response to grief was anger and despair. He was being honest with his feelings and because he was openhearted, he could later be healed of his pain.

Gideon. When his people were oppressed by the Midianites, Gideon was called to lead them to freedom. He was angry because of the pain of slavery and the separation from loved ones. The angel of Yahweh called him and told him that God was with him in his trial. Gideon dared to doubt the angel:

Forgive me, my lord, but if Yahweh is with us, then why is it that all this is happening to us now? And where are all the wonders our ancestors tell us of when they say, 'Did not Yahweh bring us out of Egypt?' But now Yahweh has deserted us; he has abandoned us . . . .

Jdg. 6: 13

Gideon was bold to be so frank. His grieving took the form of doubting God and God loved his honesty and gave him a sign of his nearness.

Naomi. She lost her husband and two sons. She grieved by wanting to be alone. She succeeded in pushing away from her one of her daughters-in-law and almost discouraged the other, Ruth, to do the same. Naomi told her:

> You must return . . . why come with me?
>
> Rt. 1:11

Naomi felt she needed privacy. This was a perfectly legitimate right — even if her comforters were so sincere.

Finally, the example of not just a holy person, but of the Son of God: Jesus of Nazareth. He mourned the death of his good friend, Lazarus. He was direct and simple with his emotions:

> Jesus wept; and the Jews said, 'See how much he loved him!'
>
> Jn. 11:35-36

We have no account of Jesus mourning the death of his stepfather, Joseph, but we can assume, I think, that his response would be similar to that of any human being who lost someone dear: pain of loss, brokenheartedness, missing the loved one. Jesus exemplifies everything that is most human.

Actually, Jesus and the others embody a particular aspect of grief. Grief can be defined as *the emotional pain of absence from a loved one*. People of faith must mourn too. Our faith does not mean that we are assured of loving without the pain of loss when we lose those we love. Nor does it mean that our mourning is something we can control. Just as with all the examples of faithful people mentioned above, we too must *express* that pain of loss.

Each of us is human in a very complex way. We like to think of ourselves as simple, uncomplicated individuals. We like to assure ourselves that we know ourselves. But we don't — not completely. We are made not only in the genetic pattern of our parents, but in the image and likeness of God. He is the Truth; we are too. And we are anything but uncomplicated. There are things going on inside of us, things that will not be acknowledged until our parents die. We are more complex than we care to admit. Grieving is a very complex process that reveals to us some of our previously unknown depth.

For this reason, it is very important *not to judge ourselves while we are grieving.* We are called to be our own best friend — not an inquisitor. Grief will open up many unpleasant feelings. These feelings are neither good nor bad. They are just ours. We are neither good nor bad for having them. We are only mourning.

Remember: we are grieving because of what is happening to us, not because of what happened to our dead loved ones. In a paradoxical way, they still live in us — their love, their values, examples, etc. It is we, the living, who have died. All of our love for them has gone into eternity with them.

Grief has a character of its own and is expressed differently by each of us. Much depends on our personality structure and our social situation (married, single, etc.). Psychiatrists do find, however, that there are certain observable stages of grief:[1]

1) The *shock* of loss itself: "I'm sorry, your father passed away a half hour ago." It does not register. We are still on automatic pilot: "Oh, thank you . . ."

2) The *numbing effect* of the shock: "Oh, no!" or "What?" Denial and disbelief as well as defense mechanisms are activated. "I don't believe it!"

[1]We are indebted to Dr. David K. Switzer's treatment of this subject in his *Dynamics of Grief* (Abingdon Press, 1970).

3) The *struggle between fantasy and reality:* "I just said to mom this morning that when she gets paroled from here we will take that trip to Florida. Maybe . . . maybe I should hold off on those plans now?"

4) The *breakthrough* and flood of grief: "It just dawned on me that he's really *dead.* I won't see him again. I miss him terribly."

5) Later, *selective memory* and the occasional stabbing pains: "I was sitting in that chair of hers and I remember the time she learned how serious dad's condition was. It was always like her to think of others first."

6) *Acceptance:* when we can let the dead influence us again. This is an ongoing stage, never finished. Some accept their parents' death but remain vulnerable to their memories for years. They describe their feelings like this: "I know my folks are dead, but I still feel sad. There is much I'd like to share with them and I know I can't. John started school today. Mom would have liked to see him off."

We all take different roads to arrive at acceptance. We all travel at different speeds. *We must mourn our own way* — not to fill the expectations of others, not even to fulfill our own expectations of what is mature and appropriate. This is a revolutionary experience in our lives. *Be honest about what you feel.* That is the one principle to follow.

Usually, we know when we are moving through the stages of grief by the diminishing degree of intensity in the symptoms.

The *symptoms:* grieving people truly suffer from a disease which has observable characteristics. Freud compared grieving with the psychological condition known to him as *melancholia.* We have difficulty realizing that we are not responsible for what we feel. Guilt is the demon that will complicate our mourning. The symptoms of grief are not pretty. We find ourselves not approving of what we are feeling. We will want to think of ourselves as being "better than that" or "beyond that" type of thought or feeling. Our picture of ourselves will be changed. It can be terrifying. It is good to remember these words:

> *Happy* those who mourn: they *shall* be comforted.

Mt. 5:5

Here is a list of reactions that people who mourn report to their doctors, clergy and friends. Far from being "abnormal," these feelings are most natural. They are a mixture of many emotions and none have a moral tint or IQ. All have one thing in common: they hurt.

1) *Extreme self-centeredness.* This is a defense against the fear of losing more of ourselves. It is often mistaken for selfishness. Part of us has died with our parents and we want to take "good care" of what is left. Any kind of demand or responsibility seems too much of an imposition. We go on strike. We don't go out of our way. We don't maintain a customary level of activity. We want to be left alone.

2) *Loss of meaning.* What used to be very important to us is not so important now. Our friendships, work, hobbies, spiritual disciplines all seem quite irrelevant. We feel empty, dead and without enthusiasm.

3) *Difficulty concentrating.* It is a chore to read a few lines in the newspaper, to do bills, to carry on a conversation. We are easily distracted and do anything to escape regimentation. We indulge our appetites.

Sleep is either difficult to find or to stay away from.

4) *Depression*. This is the most burdensome symptom. If we came from a strict upbringing, we may be more prone to this symptom than any other. It is characterized by despair, dejection, inactivity, inattention to external stimuli, detachment, feelings of exhaustion and weeping.

5) *Hostility*. Feelings of anger, even rage, at the dead for dying, at ourselves for feeling the way we do, at God (terrible as that might seem) for allowing "all this to happen." We might even strike out at those who reach out to comfort us.

6) *Guilt*. Feeling that these feelings are wrong and that we are bad for acting on them or even having them. We feel ashamed of ourselves for not being "more grown-up." For proud people, this can be humiliating and excruciatingly painful.

> For huge as the sea is your affliction; who
> can possibly cure you?
>
> *Lm. 2:13*

As noted earlier, each mourner proceeds in his or her own way. Not all the symptoms will pertain to everyone. We help ourselves by realistically accepting ourselves as the people Jesus spoke of in the Beatitudes: "Happy" (another translation reads "Blessed") "those who mourn . . . They shall be comforted." That *shall* implies future tense. It takes time.

There is no cure for mourning except to mourn. It is also helpful during this time to find someone to talk with, someone who has had the experience of losing loved ones and will not be shocked at our honesty. It also helps to talk honestly, not piously, with God. He is much larger than our feelings and is working to heal us through the grieving process. Then too, talking with the dead directly can be a great release from frustration, guilt and anger. Be verbal. Get the pain out of the heart.

Jesus said it all about mourning and where it leads to when he said:

> I tell you most solemnly, you will be weeping and wailing while the world will rejoice; you will be sorrowful, but your sorrow will turn to joy . . . You are sad now, but I shall see you again, and your hearts will be full of joy, and that joy no one shall take from you.
>
> *Jn. 16:20-23*

CHAPTER FOUR:
Forgiving God

The thought is guilt-provoking to verbalize and seems blasphemous: forgive God? Who are *we* to forgive *God?* He is all good: we are less than that. How dare we presume any right to absolve the Almighty!

But in mourning, we do trust God with our anger. Many good, believing, humble people get to the point in their grief where they blame or attack God and then burden themselves with guilt. Some can never forgive themselves for having to forgive God.

First, let us talk about *anger*. It is an emotion; it is there, part of our equipment — along with compassion, joy, jealousy, etc. God is sensibly economical. He wastes nothing; he is not excessive with anything. Whatever emotions we have, we need to have or they would not be there.

Our problem is not with anger, but with our feelings about anger. We were never taught to deal with it — only to feel guilty about it. Parents are allowed to be angry with children, but if children are angry with parents, it is disobedience, disrespect or arrogance. It is breaking the Fourth Commandment. As grown-ups, anger is one of the "Seven

Deadly Sins.'' Year after year, incident by incident, we are conditioned to feel badly about ourselves when we are angry.

It is not surprising then that whenever we feel hostile, no matter toward whom, we punish ourselves by remembering all the negative self-feelings we have learned to associate with this emotion.

Anger is not the opposite of love. We can be angry at others and still love them. We can be angry with ourselves and still respect ourselves. We can be angry with children or spouse and still love them dearly. We can even be angry with God and be his loving child. We can, amidst our rage, pray:

> Yes, Yahweh is good; his love is everlasting;
> his faithfulness endures from age to age.
>
> Ps. 105:5

When suffering is prolonged, even a person of faith is brought to realize that his basic yes to God is bounded by a multitude of no's; that his love of God is mingled with several other emotions. Pain reveals the ambivalence of human faith.

To be angry and to be able to express it is humanizing. To be afraid of it and afraid to ''let it out'' is crippling and very uncomfortable. We can use anger constructively: it can be an effective means of communicating pain. I am *hurt* — I reveal that hurt in anger.

Mature people get hurt. Sensitive people get hurt. Jesus did. And Jesus got very angry. He used anger frequently. Read any of his attacks on the doctors of the Law *(Mt. 23:13-32)* or his wrath toward unbelievers whose hearts were hard *(Mt. 11:20-24).* Remember how he cursed the fig tree in a fit of temper *(Mt. 21:18ff)* or his behavior in clearing out the Temple of those who had made it a market-place *(Mk. 11:15-19)*.

Jesus did not love less because he showed his anger. People who love each other very much use this emotion to cleanse themselves of accumulated hurts.

In the death of our parents, or of any loved one, we feel deprived. We are hurt. Sometimes, God is the only one to whom we will express our true disappointment and fury. Rather than being a source of guilt, expressing anger toward God can be seen as an honest revelation of pain. To tell God we are angry with him for "all this" is not saying we don't love him as much as it is saying that we trust him enough to listen "to it all."

God is larger than our ire. Always, he is so much bigger-hearted than we can imagine.

"I call you friends" — his words. If we only feel anger toward God but do not dare to express it, does that make us more respectful? Does it make the anger less real? Do we forget that he reads the heart, not the lips:

> The word is not even on my tongue,
> Yahweh, before you know all about it.
>
> *Ps. 139:4*

God understands the pain of separation. This is the reason he became man, the reason for salvation — to end the terrible distance between himself and us, to bring us closer to him than before. Why do we act as if God is beyond our experience when he took so much trouble to identify himself with us?

I was furious with God. I knew he did not "give" my mother cancer nor was he responsible for her slow death. I knew he was not testing her for she had been a friend of his all her life — through good times and bad. I knew he was not playing with my father during those hours on the Bennet Respirator 101. But I was angry with him for letting it happen.

In the past, I was very polite in my prayer. I was careful to place myself in a reverent attitude when coming into the Lord's presence. In other words, I "dressed up." Never would I come with my naked emotions *as they were being revealed to me* and say to God: "This is my prayer. This is the most honest expression of the depth of who I am now. I can offer no other." But in my time of exasperation, when many of my "controls" were cracking under the strain, that is exactly what I did: "End it! End it!" I ranted at heaven, "You only let your son endure a few hours of torment. Why must I go through so much more?" But heaven was silent and that made things worse.

Abandonment. Not only were my parents dying, leaving me, but God was too.

Lo! Others, holier than I, have felt the same way:

> How much longer will you forget me, Yahweh? For ever? How much longer will you hide your face from me? How much longer must I endure grief in my soul, and sorrow in my heart by day and by night?
>
> *Ps. 13:1-2*

> And that is why I weep; my eyes dissolve in tears, since the comforter who could revive me is far away.
>
> *Lm. 1:16*

> Wake up, Lord! Why are you asleep? Awake! Do not abandon us for good. Why

do you hide your face, and forget we are
wretched and exploited?

Ps. 44:23-24

Eli, Eli, lama sabachthani? . . . My God, my
God, why have you deserted me?

Mt. 27:45-46

This is the source of our anger at God. We feel
that we are left alone to face our troubles. God is
unable or unwilling to intervene. We pray for a healing or a miracle and it does not come. We blame
ourselves for a lack of faith and that convicts us in
our poor self-image even more. God's silence is
deafening and we resent it.

God's weakness is stronger than human
strength.

1 Cor. 1:25

But only in eternity is this worked out. God's defini-
tion of power is not the same as ours. He is the God
whose power is perfected in weakness. He came into
the world as a helpless baby and he left as the Lamb
of God.

Lamb: not tiger nor lion. I was angry at the way
God chose to be God. In this state of mind, I forgot,
I did not want to see all the past kindness or real
goodness that my Heavenly Father had shown me.

I forgot that he is a God of life and that he wants
no one to die:

Death was not God's doing, he takes no
pleasure in the extinction of the living. To be
— for this he created all.

Wis. 1:13

He is a God, not of the dead, but of the living.

Mk. 12:27

I have come so that they may have life.

Jn. 10:10

I forgot that he is always faithful to us and to his promises:

> Does a woman forget her baby at the breast,
> or fail to cherish the son of her womb?
>
> Yet even if these forget, I will never forget you. See, I have branded you on the palms of my hands.

Is. 49:15-16

> If my father and mother desert me, Yahweh will care for me still.

Ps. 27:10

> And know that I am with you always; yes, to the end of time.

Mt. 28:20

I had forgotten that God was still involved in the suffering of the world and that he was suffering along with my parents:

> I was sick and you visited *me*.

Mt. 25:36

He was suffering with me in my suffering too. Because God loves me, he is affected by what happens to me. Characteristic of his goodness, he makes our pain his pain. He takes the crosses of our lives onto himself in his persistent and enduring, yet quiet care for us. He draws so little attention to himself. God is a fellow-traveller.

One way I overcame my hostility toward God was to express it. In time, I heard myself talk and realized how foolish I sounded. I got tired of being angry. I began to think of God as one who suffered a loss along with me. My loss was his loss too. Death is

God's enemy too. Realizing this made me feel closer to him. As St. Paul said:

> . . . and the last of the enemies to be destroyed is death.

1 Cor. 15:25

Hope, mine and God's, relieved anger. The power of faith in the resurrection is the center of true hope and all peace. Without that hope, we are sad indeed and the most pitiable of people.

I have reflected on the Lord's resurrection of Lazarus from the dead only to let him die later. Is that what I wanted for my parents? A miracle to bring them back until I was finally ready for them to go? And would that have been enough "extra" time? No. We never have enough time with our loved ones. No time is a good time for them to die.

It is the paradox of grief: we can be happy for the dead because their pain is ended, but the end of their pain is the continuation of our own. The belief in the resurrection does not short-circuit the hurt of loss. It does keep a broken heart company and gives it reasons to be happy — in time.

I see now that the pain of loss distorts the truth about everything: the importance of the pain, the goodness and nearness of God and the value of life. When suffering, it is easy to forget that earthly life is not the absolute value; everlasting life is. In suffering, I did not realize the magnitude nor meaning of my grief. Sorrow dwarfs the vision and the spirit. Death puts us on the defensive! In this posture, we miss a lot.

I am no longer angry with God. I know he was never angry with me for my reaction, just as I would never take seriously the anger of another who was hurt. If I who am a sinner can understand, how much more so God?

> Is there a man among you who would hand his son a stone when he asked for bread? Or would hand him a snake when he asked for a fish? If you, then, who are evil, know how to give to your children what is good, how much more will your Father in heaven give good things to those who ask him!
>
> *Mt. 7:9-11*

Without a doubt, it was the loneliest of isolations not to have a sense of God. I have been to the edge of the pit and have seen the terror of despair, a life without God.

> When my heart had been growing sourer with pains shooting through my loins, I had simply failed to understand, my stupid attitude to you was brutish.
>
> *Ps. 73:21-22*

It comes down to trust — trusting that God is good no matter what the external events seem to indicate. To my eyes, my parents were dying terrible deaths. To God's, they were being transfigured, being made ready for the rest of time. It took as long (or as brief) as it had to take. I have come to believe, accept and be grateful for this.

In the post-mortem, someone sent me a home-made greeting card. On the outside was just my first name. On the inside, this simple message: "I love you. God."

I found it difficult to believe then. But God's love is always beyond understanding. Now, to soothe myself, I turn to Isaiah and as I read, I imagine that

God speaks these mighty words directly into the crevices of my life. He says:

> I will heal *you* and console *you*,
> I will comfort *you* to the full, both *you* and *your family*; bringing praise to *your* lips.
> Peace, peace to far and near, I will indeed heal *you*.

Is. 57:18-20

CHAPTER FIVE:
New Identities

In our age of instant replay, instant analysis and fast foods, we take the complexity of life for granted. We lose the patience to probe beyond the easy and obvious. TV news, satellite coverage, the "specialist's" report — all make everything seem immediate and understandable. No person is invisible to the camera, no distance too great to conquer for a sporting event, no fact beyond human knowledge. Science is our guardian and security. It will provide for our needs and satisfy all our questions. There is no room for doubt, awe or wonder except at the cleanliness of Disneyland: how *do* they keep that place so spotless?

We live within ourselves and only become familiar with the shell.

But there is a question that lives within us. It has a small yet persistent voice: "Who am I?" We fear to shout this question out loud, to admit that there is something so basic that has not been completely explained by science or culture. We distract ourselves from the lack of resolution by either keeping too busy or by giving ourselves an obvious answer. But no matter how we avoid the inevitable confrontation, we cannot go on our way till we deal with it effectively. "Who am I, really?" It is not easily answered and we have a classroom of guesses:

"I am a man," "I am a wife," "I am a member of this community," "I am an American," "I am a child of God," "I am a friend," "I am a teacher."

Is any as old as: "I am a son"; "I am a daughter"?

Human beings are rivers, not blocks of marble. As we flow through time, we acquire a self-concept — an image or understanding of ourselves. We tend to get stuck in that self-image and, in a sense, we become our own institution and way of life. Often, when we think of ourselves, we can only think of others to whom we are related or those from whom we are given titles or names.

For the longest time, we have looked to our parents to tell us who we are and who we are not. Their very existence has also made it possible for us to make evaluations about our relationship to the future:

We are not as old as they; we have time to accomplish our plans;

We are stronger of breath, step and arm;

We are not as close to death as they;

We are following them into the future — they go first, then us;

We are not the next to die.

But when they die, much of what we thought about ourselves is challenged. Our securities and illusions about immortality vanish. We become our own link with the future. They have stepped aside and we cannot stand behind them on the time line any longer. We face death head-on.

The death of our parents shakes up the institutional self-understanding. The oldest and first learned role no longer functions the way it did in the past. A basic component in our self-awareness is missing. As long as they live, part of us has never had to grow up; part of us could always think of itself as "child" — a little dependent and a little helpless.

We are more helpless than we would like to admit in our age of certainty.

At this critical time in our lives, our self-understanding is like the dew. Notice how dew never permeates the grass. It catches light, shimmers, makes the grass sheen with circles of small suns, but it does not nourish nor moisten the roots. Dew burns away by noontime. So too, our self-understanding at various times in our lives; it is subject to change. What is only meant to be temporary has reached its limitations. Something else must take its place.

The transition in self-image is often very radical and traumatic. Trauma is defined as:

> Any injury, wound or shock, most frequently structural, but also mental, in the form of an emotional shock producing a disturbance, more or less enduring, of mental functions.[1]

The death of our parents is such an experience. We have been saying that it takes time for the wound to heal, the shock to be absorbed, the functions to return to clarity.

But when the dust settles, we will not feel the same way about ourselves. We will never be able to think of ourselves in exactly the same way — unless we persist in denying the reality of our parents' death and that would be to live an unhealthy fantasy.

[1]*Dictionary of Psychology* (Penguin, 1974) p. 303.

We are more than any *one* role. We are more than any one *name*. We are not defined by any *single* relationship. The real self is the one which exists in and through all the roles we play. The grand illusion is to think of ourselves as being just who we say we are or want ourselves to be.

The basic self goes on after the termination of any specific role. It maintains itself. Separation from loved ones does not reduce us, but it does change the way we look at ourselves.

It is a law of nature that when something is lacking or taken away, the resulting imbalance demands a corresponding compensation. But when our parents die, no "corresponding compensation" exists. If a spouse dies, it is possible to marry again. We only have one set of parents; they are irreplaceable. There are no substitutions for those who raised us. We share too much history with them.

The death of our parents leaves spaces in our identities. Lao Tze, a contemporary of Confucius, reflects on the constructive use of spaces:

> Thirty spokes share one hub. Adapt the empty spaces therein to the purpose at hand, and you will have the use of the cart. Knead the clay in order to make a vessel. Adapt the empty spaces to the purpose at hand, and you will have the use of the vessel. . .
>
> Thus what we gain is Something, yet it is by virture of Nothing that this can be put to use.[2]

Who are we? In faith, beloved of God our Father. Subjectively, our feelings. We are our feel-

[2]*Lao Tze/Tao Te Ching* (Penguin Books, 1963), p. 67.

ings. These are the elements of ourselves.

When parents die, many feelings emerge that were not permitted to surface while they were living. We hid them. We did not allow ourselves to experience many feelings because we knew, or presumed, that our parents would not approve. They would be shocked, disappointed.

In many ways, their death is an act of liberation for the parts of ourselves that we have denied all these years. We need not be afraid of these feelings. They are not enemies, only strangers.

A new awareness of self is being born. New pieces of our personal puzzle become available to us and slowly fall into place. An internal pattern of old and new is discovered.

Because we are so easily frightened by what we do not understand, we are tempted to "stay the same," to deny growth, to short-circuit our mourning and our freedom at the same time. We want to tell our feelings what they ought to be rather than learn from them. We want to deny some of them as too foreign to us. We are "too old" or "too tired" to start thinking about ourselves in a different light.

For those who are patient, false fronts get dropped, masks are stripped away. We face ourselves with fewer deceptions, fictions and obstacles. We see deeper into our unsettled regions and learn that we have a frontier! We now get beyond the conventional and realize that so much of our life has been guided by what we thought we should be or what we thought our parents expected us to be.

We might discover that their approval motivated us to pursue things we no longer wish to do.

Have we lived only in response to their hidden

demands, programmed into our upbringing? Has duty, obligation, responsibility been chosen by us or have we accepted a collection of functions that go with the "job" as they knew it?

Do we make changes now that we see more of who we are and want to be? Can we be this honest with ourselves? Are the consequences so terrifying? Can we respond to the truth of our feelings? Can we trust ourselves — no matter how long we have been dependent on our parents for unspoken directions?

These are questions of the first order which lead us to the possibility of identity reorganization.

Reorganization. We see the necessity of making new sense out of our lives. We need to integrate the new information about who we are and who we want to be. We make adjustments in our attitudes toward ourselves and many aspects of our normal, everyday living. We meet new meanings, discover new needs. Hopefully, we take the opportunity to interpret ourselves to ourselves. To do this, we need a value system. Taking the best from the system our parents gave us, we can regroup responsibly rather than recklessly. To say: "Well, I can do now whatever I want to do — no matter what" is to speak like a child still. Rather, it is healthier to say: "What I have learned plus what I have been taught brings me to these changes." Our new identities are more likely to be satisfying if they are products of reflection rather than rebellion.

We are free to make ourselves more the person God calls us to be. Sincere persons use freedom to better respond to the Lord's call: "Be perfect," that is, *"be whole."*

Reentry into routine will be a slow, and for some time, reluctant process. We may have to

56

establish new routines to accompany our new identities. Maybe we will find ourselves pulling back from many commitments. Perhaps we will want to "go out" of ourselves more than in the past. People who knew us for years may detect changes in us without being able to identify them. Some will not like the "new" model. They would have us be consistent, stay the same, not cross over any lines. They would have us be the way we were *before trauma* — as if nothing had really happened. When we change, we are difficult to relate to; we challenge others to examine themselves.

It is necessary to talk out loud and boldly about these modifications we are making. We can use an objective listener to help us identify the genuine conversions that are taking place and point out the superficial changes — the possible fads we will also experience during this time. The simple key is to speak honestly, completely honestly, with someone we trust.

It is also healthy to form new relationships with the people who share our new interests. The emerging self needs fellowship and support to grow. Nurture the newness. Invest time and love in the project of becoming who you are and see how peaceful life can be.

The death of our parents is one of the major revolutions of our lives. God said:

Now I am making the whole of creation new.

Rv. 21:5

And he is doing his work through our attempts to make new identities for ourselves. It is holy work. It is sacred activity. Yet it is sloppy and never final. It can be lonely and painful. It is exciting. It is taking responsibility for our own being-in-the-world. We are now continuing the process that God and our parents began at our conception.

God has created us and God will care for us: the new self as well as the old. He loved us as innocent babes even before we knew who we were. He loves us through all the subsequent changes. No trial, no loss ever changes the perfection of his great love. He bids us to do what we have to do in confidence and says:

> Do not be afraid, for I have redeemed you;
> I have called you by your name, you are
> mine.
> Should you pass through the sea, I will be
> with you; or through rivers, they will not
> swallow you up. Should you walk through
> fire, you will not be scorched and the
> flames will not burn you.
> For I am Yahweh, your God, the Holy
> One of Israel, your saviour.

Is. 43:2-3

CHAPTER SIX:
Remembering Our Deceased Loved Ones With Joy

Wakes concluded. Funeral Rites ended. Relatives and friends gone back to the routines interrupted by death. Everyone very tired. Turn on the television for distraction from the intensity of these days, these events. A hundred memories compete with what is on the screen for our attention. All of a sudden, we find ourselves weeping. Remembering our parents hurts so much.

> It is not a turtle hiding in its little green shell.
> It is not a stone to pick up and put under
>   your black wing.
> It is not a subway car that is obsolete.
> It is not a lump of coal that you could light.
> It is a dead heart.
> It is inside of me.
> It is a stranger yet once it was agreeable,
>   opening and closing like a clam.[1]

Some choose not to remember. They exhaust themselves walling in the pain they are afraid to touch. They must sleep sometime. Their dreams, then, will remember the dead.

[1]Anne Sexton, "The Dead Heart" in *The Awful Rowing Toward God*, (Houghton Mifflin Co., 1975), p. 36.

It is better to remember and weep. Faith and hope will keep our dead, broken hearts company.

> They went away, went away weeping,
>   carrying the seed;
> they come back, come back singing,
>   carrying their sheaves.

Ps. 126:5b-6

Peter and the Apostles remembered Jesus after the events of Good Friday and they wept. Mary, his mother and Mary Magdalene did too. Good Friday is more than a twenty-four hour stretch. It is a wound that takes time to heal. Remembering is the pain and the medicine. Remembering our dead ones gives us more time with them, sustains the relationship. It is our way of reaching out into eternity to be with them. It is our conquering their death.

Memory is stronger than death. In remembering, we are not merely "holding on," we are *creating* space in our lives for the new shape of the relationship: the eternal dimension.

> We all know that *something* is eternal. And it ain't houses and it ain't even names, and it ain't even the stars — everybody knows in their bones that *something* is eternal and that *something* has to do with human beings. There is something way down deep that's eternal about every human being.[2]

Unlike the machines and gadgets of our day, people are designed to last forever. People — not just their bodies — are made of cosmic stuff. Memories of them not only are psychic remains of how they were, but that they were and are. We do

[2]Thornton Wilder, *Our Town*, Act III.

not only remember the last days of their lives — usually the most painful and unhappy — but all the years, rich with many good times. These, the good times, are just as real as the hurtful ones.

I think we weep when we remember them because we long to be immortal with them. Yes, we miss them, but we do not want to bring them back here. We want to be where they are, where the saints are:

> Welcome into your kingdom our departed brothers and sisters, and all who have left this world in your friendship. There we hope to share in your glory when every tear will be wiped away. On that day we shall see you, our God, as you are. We shall become like you and praise you forever . . . .
>
> *Eucharistic Prayer III*

Remembering with pain is suffering. Let us be clear about this. It is a continuation of the effect of death. It is not a lack of faith in the resurrection nor a doubting of God's mercy. As suffering, it is one of the ways we are brought to see deeper truths about life. Oscar Wilde, the English playwright said:

> . . . people who use phrases without wisdom sometimes talk of suffering as a mystery. It is really a revelation. One discerns things that are never discerned before. One approaches the whole of human history from a different standpoint.[3]

St. Paul suffered. He saw the Lord in everything. To live, he said, was Christ. And more, his suffering made him miss Jesus so much he wanted to die:

[3]Oscar Wilde, *De Profundis* (Avon Books, 1963 ed) p. 128.

> I want to be gone and be with Christ,
> which would be very much the better . . . .
>
> *Phil. 1:23*

But Paul also had hope. He admonished his fellow Christians to grieve for the dead, but not like those who have no hope. Translated: remember your dead loved ones, miss them, but do not jump into the grave with them because in the end we will be one in Christ.

In another place, Paul speaks of the kind of agony endured in waiting to be rejoined with Christ and those who have gone before us:

> In this present state, it is true, we groan as
> we wait with longing to put on our
> heavenly home over the other . . . Yes,
> we groan and find it a burden being still
> in this tent . . . .
>
> *2 Cor. 5:2-4*

Memories are more than clouds in the sky — one moment there, large as mountains, the next moment gone. No, memories are benedictions we bestow, tributes we pay to all the love we have given and received. Not to remember is not to have cared.

Memories are like dry bones that can be breathed into by love to raise a chorus of gratitude to our parents. Those memories are living flames to give us warmth. We need not live in the fire, only return to it when we are cold. It will always be there. It is a legacy. It is our Old Testament.

Christianity is based on remembering Christ: his life, death and resurrection. Jesus was very insistent that his followers remember him and act accordingly: "Do this, in memory of me."

We thank you for all the blessings you gave
them in this life time to show your fatherly
care for all of us . . . .

Rite of Christian Burial

Remembering is nature's way of reducing the
sense of powerlessness created by such radical
surgery of our feelings. It alleviates the sense of loss
rather than increases it.

We stand like visitors at a boat-dock, watching a
ship make its way into the ceiling of the horizon. In-
stinctively, we say, "There she goes." We leave the
dock with a sense of loss, of absence. We forget that
on the other end of that voyage is another dock and
spectators who will say: "Here she comes."
Something for them is completed.

That is our memory for the dead — relating to
the other side of their voyage.

Memory brings us into the future! We must
remember if we are to tell the future.

We all can remember the beauty of a Spring day.
It is that memory that enables us to take heart and
endure the Winter. Remembering what has been,
gives us hope to anticipate what has to come. No
Winter lasts forever. We may be humbled by cold
and ice, but we never seriously doubt that April and
May are coming and that they will be like all other
Springs we have known. So God says:

Stop your weeping, dry your eyes, your
hardships will be redressed.

Jer. 31:16

The memories of our parents are, through the
tears, ultimately restorative. God addresses us
through them and joins us to our family.

As I write this book, I am living in the house my parents lived in for the past eleven years. Each room is a chalice, holding their tastes, echoes of their voices and traces of their laughter. Everything seems only temporarily abandoned, yet it has been two years since they have died. It is like yesterday. It is like it never happened — the hospitals, pain, waiting, deaths, wakes, funerals, weeping. Death has given the house a timelessness and a gentle, expectant quiet. Something of them persists here.

It was once very difficult to be here. I was afraid of the associations. Now, I see them as helping me to remember.

At this moment, I sit at the kitchen table, in the chair my mother never occupied for too long as she darted to and from the stove to serve my father and me. His chair is to my right. It is still and modest, open and supportive — not unlike my father's disposition.

I can remember my parents through these things. They make me glad that I knew them.

Outside, in the cold November morning, the sun shines on the sleeping garden they planted and carefully tended. They enjoyed noticing things grow. I do too. It is one of the gifts they left me. My mother would take her flowers to the State Hospital across the street and place the roses on the wards to bring some color and softness to the institutionality of bars and locks. That garden, now badly in need of work, is a metaphor for her loving charity and the devotion to the art of caring. Every kind act I do is, in a sense, a continuation of her kindness. Remembering her example helps keep me generous.

One special way of remembering is by praying. It is a means of joining my heart to my parents' hearts and to God's heart. The power of prayer is the power of love. I embrace my loved ones when I pray for them and even *with* them. Occasionally, my prayer will take the form of a simple imaginative bread-breaking episode. We break bread together and remember the Lord's goodness to us. Eucharist means "thanksgiving by remembering."

> *Remember* thy servants, O Lord, according to the favor which thou barest unto thy people, and grant that, increasing in knowledge and love of thee, they may go from strength to strength in the life of perfect service, in thy heavenly kingdom.
>
> Book of Common Prayer

> *Remember,* Lord, those who have died and have gone before us marked with the sign of faith, especially those for whom we now pray . . . .
>
> Eucharistic Prayer I

> Jesus, . . . *remember* me when you come into your kingdom.
>
> *Lk. 23:42*

It is the wonder of faith that we can face the end of our earthly life and that of others, not with fear, but courage. Only in faith could Paul write these words and only in faith can we really understand them and let them make us happy:

> When this perishable nature has put on imperishability, and when this mortal nature has put on immortality, then the words of scripture will come true: Death is swallowed

up in victory. Death, where is your victory?
Death, where is your sting?

1 Cor. 15:54-56

APPENDIX ONE:
The Origin of Death Rites and Their Significance for Those Who Mourn

Human beings are the only creatures known to bury their dead with ritual. In every culture, as far back as the Ice Age (which ended 50,000 years ago), archeology has uncovered patterned practices of dealing with the deceased members of society. From the very beginning of civilization it seems that death was treated with ritual. No one was just permitted to die. The survivors felt the need to make a response that indicated both grief and fear. Customs and practices stemmed from early man's attitudes toward life after death and toward the dead themselves.

PRE-JEWISH CUSTOMS

Death Rites were composed of a strange combination of feelings toward the dead. Primitive man both mourned and feared the recently departed. Essentially, death was viewed as a rite of passage, a transitional phase from one status of existence to another (much like puberty or marriage). In all cultures, death rites played a central role for legal as well as religious reasons as they were necessary to ascertain actual death and the subsequent disposition of the deceased's property.

Except for the Egyptian custom, bodies were usually deposited in the ground outside of inhabited areas. The dead were garbed in the clothes used during life. The corpse was either drawn together — knees to chin and laid on its left side — or stretched out on its back with arms at the sides. It was surrounded by deposits of articles used in life: dishes, bowls, pitchers, lamps, pieces of furniture, weapons, articles of adornment, food and drink. These artifacts, it was believed, would be needed for the next life.

Those who mourned their dead kept vigil for as few as seven or as many as seventy days. The purposes were different in different cultures. For example, some watched in the hope that the dead would return to life; others to guard the corpse from evil spirits; still others to provide assistance to the dead spirit in its new stage during the first confusing days after death. The Irish custom of "waking the ghost" is perhaps a vestige of attempts to bring the dead back to life through magical rites.

Coupled with the deathwatch were the practices of mourning. These were elaborate and extensive ceremonials which served two purposes: they set the mourners apart from others so that the contamination of death would not affect the community and they expressed the society's belief in the hereafter. There were long periods of mourning, loud wailing, the tearing of garments and dressing in sackcloth. Survivors would walk barefooted with heads uncovered and would neglect the ordinary care of the body. They sat on the ground, putting dust and ashes on their heads and would beat their breasts vigorously. And always, they lamented in hysterical whines that were meant to demonstrate grief and chase away evil spirits.

JEWISH CUSTOMS

The Old Testament clearly indicates that the Jews adopted death rites from the pagans and adapted them to their unique monotheistic religion (See: *Ecc. 38:16-24; Jer. 9:16-18).* Much of the prevailing custom influenced the burials of Abraham and Moses. Funerals were considered as obligatory as burial itself. Not to have them was considered to be a curse.

It was the responsibility of the relatives and those affected by death to attend to rites and rituals. These began at the moment of death and lasted usually seven days.

The Bible demonstrates that there was a significant evolution of the notion of the afterlife between the time of Moses and the death of the last prophet. The changing attitude toward death, of course, influenced the attitude toward the dead. The early Old Testament writings held (as did the pagan) that all the dead, regardless of social position or moral character, went to Sheol. This realm, described as being under the earth, was portrayed as an eternal house with chambers, rooms and gates. It was a prison with bars and bolts. It was said to be the land of oblivion from which none returned. The Jews often paralleled Sheol with "the pit," the grave; when the earth is opened for burial, the grave is the entrance to Sheol. It was called "No More" and was in no way a positive state of survival after life — rather a place of eternal inactivity. A soul in Sheol was in "suspended animation." Though Yahweh

controlled the region, those there did not thank him
nor were they close to him *(Is. 38:18; Ps. 6:6)*.

The later Old Testament, however, expresses a
belief in resurrection and immortality. There was
also a strong current of belief that the fate of the dead
would depend on virtue or the lack of it during life.
Thus, death was not feared because it would
automatically end in the oblivion of darkness but
because the judgment of God would follow.

EARLY CHRISTIAN CUSTOMS

In the life of the early Church, burial customs
continued Jewish practices (See: *Mk. 5:22-24; Lk.
7:11-15; Acts 9:36-42)*. There was one dramatic exception: the belief in the resurrection of Jesus
changed the attitude toward death *completely*. Christian burial rites stressed the reverence due the body
as the creation of God and Temple of the Holy
Spirit. The body was also treated with reverence
because of the future glory it would share with the
resurrected Christ.

The procedure, carried out by the family, has
been described by Augustine and other early Christian writers. With rare exception, the rites were administered as follows:

Upon ascertaining death, the eyes and mouth
were closed and the body washed. Only the Egyptian Christians practiced embalming. The ordinary
practice was to anoint the body with oil and myrrh to
preserve it for burial. The dead were then wrapped
in linen and covered by a toga and outer garments
that indicated the deceased's state of life. These were
usually violet in color.

Apparently, some of the pagan excesses of adorning the body crept into Christian practices as the early Fathers often criticized their flocks for using precious apparel of silk and gold for burial. This was thought to be a vain display which drew attention to the body and not to the new life of resurrection.

Whenever possible, a wake was held before burial in the home of the deceased, but more frequently there was a three-day watch at the grave. The wake was an occasion to console the relatives and pray for the dead. The body was surrounded, not by articles to be used in the next life, but by candles symbolizing the perpetual light to which the dead are called. Priests would read Scripture passages, psalms were sung (the favorites being: *Ps. 22, 31, 100, 114, 115)* and there was exhortation about the hope of New Life. Pagan practices were forbidden: no instrumental music, no hired mourners, no actors or jesters.

After the brief mourning period, on the third day after death, there was a Triumphal Funeral Procession to the place where a Mass would be celebrated. This was usually a church but records also state that the cemetery was used for this event. The head of the departed was uncovered and raised up in anticipation of the resurrection. Acolytes preceded the entourage; bishops and priests carried the bodies of outstanding persons followed by the family and friends. The victorious spirit exhibited by the Christians amazed the pagans!

St. John Chrysostom explained: ''Is it not that we praise God and thank him that he has crowned the departed and freed him from suffering, and that God has the deceased now freed from fear in Himself?''

At the conclusion of the Eucharist, a funeral oration, not a eulogy, was offered by a relative or friend of the dead. Essentially, the focus of these remarks was exhortation: look to the Everlasting Light, remember the Lord who has gone before you to New Life, do not be downcast.

Before departing from the place of burial, the relatives imparted the final kiss, a gesture of affection and respect. Then the body was buried facing East — awaiting the coming of the *Son* in glory. Upon leaving the cemetery, all gave a last farewell: *Vivas,* "You live," a prayer that the dead might live on in God and intercede for the living.

Visits to the cemetery were frequent and special anniversaries were commemorated on the third, seventh, ninth, thirteenth and fortieth years after death.

MODERN CUSTOM

In the *Constitution on the Sacred Liturgy* (#81 and footnote #53) the Church Fathers of Vatican II stated:

> The rite for the burial of the dead should evidence more clearly the paschal character of Christian death, and should correspond more closely to the circumstances and traditions found in various regions.
>
> The traditional rites for Christian burial have been too often expressive of gloom rather than of the paschal mystery. Christ's resurrection and our own entrance into His Life and resurrection should be the themes of Christian death and its ritual expression.

Thus, the Bishops hoped to restore the emphasis on New Life that had been the original focus of the Christian Death Rite but which had fallen into sad disfavor after the third century.

The remnants of the early customs have returned. The reverence and devotion bestowed on the body are based on the belief of the corporeal resurrection according to which the body is destined to enjoy happiness with God forever. Accordingly, the priest wears white vestments, the coffin is draped with a white pall, the *Alleluia* is sung before the Gospel and the Easter Candle — symbol of the Risen Christ's presence with his people — burns in the presence of the dead as well.

The purpose of the wake and burial rite are the same today as then. In a publication of the American Conference of Catholic Bishops entitled *The Guidelines for Christian Burial,* a reaffirmation of the spirit of renewal and restoration of the earlier custom is asserted:

> The community of relatives, friends and parishioners comes together to provide its prayerful support; the whole Christian community through the Church and its liturgy offers its prayers for God's mercy on the deceased and His strength for the bereaved.

In the words of the Ritual itself, these are the final remarks of the Commendation and Farewell:

> Father, into your hands we commend our brother. We are confident that with all who have died in Christ he will be raised to life on the last day and live with Christ forever. We thank you for all the blessings you gave him

in this life to show your fatherly care for all of us and the fellowship which is ours with the saints in Jesus Christ.

Lord, hear our prayer: welcome our brother to paradise and help us to comfort each other with the assurance of our faith until we all meet in Christ to be with you and with our brother forever.

Perhaps the most striking departure from custom is that most of what was done by the family is now done by professional morticians and their staffs. Still, the pattern of funeral rites follows the pattern of Christianity itself: they begin in suffering and end in joy.

A Collection of Various Prayers for the Deceased

Prayer for a Grave Visitation

Father in Heaven,
you who make everything beautiful
and balances rhythms of winter and spring,
bless this ground
and the sleeping saints it cradles
in its long, brown fingers.
As the sun and stars shine on us,
let them not forget those who rest unseen
beneath the soft crust of earth;
let their white light be icons
of your memory for our dead;
let your rain penetrate the grass
as your grace the coverlet of silence.

Dearest Father,
help us to recall the measure of their years,
not only the day we placed them here;
help us to stretch our sorrow into recollections
of joy that will not die.
Bless the earth, Father,
and your lonely children.

Prayer for the Anniversary of a Dead Parent

Father,
a calendar is a circle
returning to its birthday.
It is like a tree
that stays the same yet changes
(imperceptibly after a while).
Today is the birthday of a saint,
my mother, my father.
Today, years ago, your glory
called them home
to sit beside your angels.
Today, we remember the birthright
of your baptized: eternity —
eternity drunk from the cup of pain.
Today, we are closer to them than yesterday
and sing alleluia for their good fortune.
Today, we stand at their feet
and yours
and offer incense of memory
to the stars — their eyes
and the sun — their joy.

Father, today you place on us
the care of remembering
that everything begins
and ends
with you.

Prayer on Disposing of Mass Cards

Dearest Father,
before me is a collection
of faith and love
folded in leather
and stamped in white gold:
Dona eis, Domine, requiem sempiternam.

These prayers have sat in darkness —
in the winter of this drawer —
like waiting seeds
or embryos
stretching their necks for fresh air.
Dust does not settle on such love.

Father,
bless the donors of these affections
and let their gifts be given back
tenfold.
Let my heart return the peace
their kindness gave to me
when life was bitter bread
and tears were hot and long.

**Prayer to Be Said on Finding
an Object Dear to the Deceased**

Father,
all life is a network of threads
connecting us to one another
and to you.
Memory is the web of tiny things
made special by someone's love.
Let me not fear this tie;
let me not fear to touch the trace
or follow it to its dear mentor.

Father,
you give us history to secure us
in our weakness;
you give us youth to grow away from;
you give us parents — Our Old Testament
to remind us of your patience.
Help me see in this small item
not a relic of the dead
but a highway to the living
who loved it
and us.

Bless this moment of wholeness,
bless it
and make us happy to remember.

Prayer of Fast — in Place of Words

Dear Father,
I regret my mute spirit.
Let my hunger rise before your lips
and kiss you for me,
say what my heart will not say.
I cannot pray.
I will not offend you
with my sad absence.
Take these hours of no-bread
as my love
or take this — my hunger,
my life —
home.

Prayer at Visiting the House They Lived in

Dear Father,
we are all tenants
on this earth
in our hollow flesh
and in our wooden dwellings.

These spaces were home to them
who made space for me to be.
Here we laughed and cried
and lived in the common hours
with peace and confidence.

Now it is empty
or filled with new residents —
a change of ownership,
sacrilege-like,
living in another's skin.

Keep our hearts wise,
dear Father.
You are their home,
You are the permanent place.
You made your camp in them on earth,
now they abide in you.

Prayer During a Painful Memory

Dear Father,
you have awarded memory
to be the king of history,
stronger than time and changing seasons.
It is the cupped hands of our past,
a holy hollow from which we drink
or quench the thirst made raw
from too much novelty.

But *this* memory is like a stone
that interrupts the comfort of my drinking
and gives me cause to rebel.

I was not always gentle
nor grateful;
I did not bring flowers
nor sing;
I took so much more
than I wanted to give.

In this pain, Father, join us
and let your mercy heal me.
Let their generosity live
and let my children take freely from me.

Memory is stronger than death
and history can repeat itself
for the good.

Prayer for Breaking Bread With the Dead

Father,
gather us about the table
of family
and sit us in warm situation
with you and one another.
Give us your bread,
consecrate it, break it,
shred it,
place it on our humble hands
that greet this nourishment
like pilgrims a new shore.
Keep our appetites holy.
Let us hold hands
and look into each other's faces.
Teach us the syllables of grace
before and after life,
a simple thanks for the yeast and dough
of all our days and nights together
and with you.

Prayer for the Back Cover of a Mass Booklet

for Natale L. Zanca
January 27, 1978

Dear Father,
the January earth
receives your broken heart
like the prodigal's father
taking him home.
Christ died again today
in your death
and his mother's weeping
nourishes your bones.
You sleep now
not alone.
Your wife warms the ground
beside you.

Let Christ, your brother,
lead you safely home.

List of Scripture References
Used in
MOURNING:
THE HEALING JOURNEY

Preface
1 Pet. 5:10
Qo. 1:4, 10
Lm. 3:25

Chapter 1
Gen. 2:24
Mt. 8:21
Mt. 10:37
Jer. 9:16-18
Jn. 6:44
I Tim. 5:4
Jn. 12:24-25

Chapter 2
Lk. 23:26
Mt. 10:38
2 Cor. 12:10
1 Cor. 1:25
Ps. 69:1-3
Jer. 10:23

Chapter 3
Ecc. 38:16-24
2 Sam. 19:1, 3&5
Jb. 3:1-4

Jdg. 6:13
Rt. 1:11
Jn. 11:35-36
Mt. 5:5
Lm. 2:13
Jn. 16:20-23

Chapter 4
Ps. 105:5
Mt. 23:13-32
Mt. 11:20-24
Mt. 21:18ff
Mk. 11:15-19
Ps. 139:4
Ps. 13:1-2
Lm. 1:16
Ps. 44:23-24
Mt. 27:45-46
1 Cor. 1:25
Wis. 1:13
Mk. 12:27
Jn. 10:10
Is. 49:15-16
Ps. 27:10
Mt. 28:20
Mt. 25:36

1 Cor. 15:25
Mt 7:9-11
Ps. 73:21-22
Is. 57:18-20

Chapter 5
Rv. 21:5
Is. 43:2-3

Chapter 6
Ps. 126:5b-6
Phil. 1:23
2 Cor. 5:2-4
Jer. 31:16
Lk. 23:42
1 Cor. 15:54-56

Appendix
Ecc. 38:16-24
Jer. 9:16-18
Is. 38:18
Ps. 6:6
Mk. 5:22
Lk. 7:11-15
Acts 9:36-42
Ps. 22
Ps. 31
Ps. 100
Ps. 114
Ps. 115

SPIRITUAL DIRECTION
Contemporary Readings   4.95

Edited by: Kevin Culligan, O.C.D. The revitalized ministry of
spiritual direction is one of the surest signs of renewal in today's Church. In this book seventeen leading writers and
spiritual directors discuss history, meaning, demands and
practice of this ministry. Readers of the book should include
not just a spiritual elite, but the entire Church — men and
women, clergy and laity, members of religious communities.

THE RETURNING SUN
Hope for a Broken World   2.50

George A. Maloney, S.J. In this collection of meditations, the
author draws on his own experiences rooted in Eastern Christianity to aid the reader to enter into the world of the "heart". It
is hoped that through contemplation of this material he/she
will discover the return of the inextinguishable Sun of the
universe, Jesus Christ, in a new and more experiential way.

LIVING HERE AND HEREAFTER
Christian Dying, Death and Resurrection   2.95

Msgr. David E. Rosage. The author offers great comfort to us
by dispelling our fears and anxieties about our life after this
earthly sojourn. Based on God's Word as presented in Sacred
Scripture, these brief daily meditations help us understand
more clearly and deeply the meaning of suffering and death.

PRAYING WITH SCRIPTURE IN THE HOLY LAND: Daily Meditations With the Risen Jesus 2.95

Msgr. David E. Rosage. Herein is offered a daily meeting with the Risen Jesus in those Holy Places which He sanctified by His human presence. Three hundred and sixty-five Scripture texts are selected and blended with the pilgrimage experiences of the author, a retreat master, and well-known writer on prayer.

DISCERNMENT: Seeking God in Every Situation 3.50

Rev. Chris Aridas. "Many Christians struggle with ways to seek, know and understand God's plan for their lives. This book is prayerful, refreshing and very practical for daily application. It is one to be read and used regularly, not just read." *Rav. Roh, O.S.B.*

A DESERT PLACE 1.95

Adolfo Quezada. "The author speaks of the desert place deep within, where one can share the joy of the Lord's presence, but also the pain of the nights of our own faithlessness." *Pecos Benedictine.*

MOURNING: THE HEALING JOURNEY 2.50

Rev. Kenneth J. Zanca. Comfort for those who have lost a loved one. Out of the grief suffered in the loss of both parents within two months, this young priest has written a sensitive, sympathetic yet humanly constructive book to help others who have lost loved ones. This is a book that might be given to the newly bereaved.

THE BORN-AGAIN CATHOLIC   3.50

Albert H. Boudreau. This book presents an authoritative imprimatur treatment of today's most interesting religious issue. The author, a Catholic layman, looks at Church tradition past and present and shows that the born-again experience is not only valid, but actually is Catholic Christianity at its best. The exciting experience is not only investigated, but the reader is guided into revitalizing his or her own Christian experience. The informal style, colorful personal experiences, and helpful diagrams make this book enjoyable and profitable reading.

WISDOM INSTRUCTS HER CHILDREN:
The Power of the Spirit and the Word   3.50

John Randall, S.T.D. The author believes that now is God's time for "Wisdom." Through the Holy Spirit, "power" has become much more accessible in the Church. Wisdom, however, lags behind and the result is imbalance and disarray. The Spirit is now seeking to pour forth a wisdom we never dreamed possible. This outpouring could lead us into a new age of Jesus Christ! This is a badly needed, most important book, not only for the Charismatic Renewal, but for the whole Church.

DISCOVERING PATHWAYS TO PRAYER   2.95

Msgr. David E. Rosage. Following Jesus was never meant to be dull, or worse, just duty-filled. Those who would aspire to a life of prayer and those who have already begun, will find this book amazingly thorough in its scripture-punctuated approach.

"A simple but profound book which explains the many ways and forms of prayer by which the person hungering for closer union with God may find Him." *Emmanuel Spillane, O.C.S.O., Abbot, Our Lady of the Holy Trinity Abbey, Huntsville, Utah.*

GRAINS OF WHEAT 2.50

Kelly B. Kelly. This little book of words received in prayer is filled with simple yet often profound leadings, exhortations and encouragement for daily living. Within the pages are insights to help one function as a Christian, day by day, minute by minute.

BREAD FOR THE EATING 2.50

Kelly B. Kelly. Sequel to the popular GRAINS OF WHEAT, this small book of words received in prayer draws the reader closer to God through the imagery of wheat being processed into bread. The author shares her love of the natural world.

DESERT SILENCE:
A Way of Prayer for an Unquiet Age 2.50

Alan J. Placa. and *Brendan Riordan.* The pioneering efforts of the men and women of the early church who went out into the desert to find union with the Lord has relevance for those of us today who are seeking the pure uncluttered desert place within to have it filled with the loving silence of God's presence.

WHO IS THIS GOD YOU PRAY TO? 2.50

Bernard Hayes, C.R. Who is God to me? How do I "picture" Him? This book helps us examine our negative images of God and, through prayer, be lead to those images which Jesus reveals to us and which can help us grow into a deeper and more valid relationship with God as Father, Lover, Redeemer, etc.

UNION WITH THE LORD IN PRAYER
Beyond Meditation to Affective Prayer Aspiration and Contemplation 1.50

Venard Polusney, O. Carm. "A magnificent piece of work. It touches on all the essential points of Contemplative Prayer. Yet it brings such a sublime subject down to the level of comprehension of the 'man in the street,' and in such an encouraging way."
Abbott James Fox, O.C.S.O. (former superior of Thomas Merton at the Abbey of Gethsemane).

ATTAINING SPIRITUAL MATURITY FOR CONTEMPLATION
(According to St. John of the Cross) 1.50

Venard Polusney, O. Carm. "I heartily recommend this work with great joy that at last the sublime teachings of St. John of the Cross have been brought down to the understanding of the ordinary Christian without at the same time watering them down. For all (particularly for charismatic Christians) hungry for greater contemplation."
George A. Maloney, S.J. Editor of Diakonia,
Professor of Patristics and Spirituality Fordham University.

PRAYING WITH MARY 2.95

Msgr. David E. Rosage. This book is one avenue which will help us discover ways and means to satisfy our longing for prayer and a more personal knowledge of God. Prayer was Mary's lifestyle. As we come to know more about her life of prayer we will find ourselves imitating her in our approach to God.

LINGER WITH ME
Moments Aside With Jesus
3.50

Rev. Msgr. David E. Rosage. God is calling us to a listening posture in prayer in the desire to experience Him at the very core of our being. Monsignor Rosage helps us to "come by ourselves apart" daily and listen to what Jesus is telling us in Scripture.

THE BOOK OF REVELATION:
What Does It Really Say?
2.50

John Randall, S.T.D. The most discussed book of the Bible today is examined by a scripture expert in relation to much that has been published on the Truth. A simply written and revealing presentation. The basis for many discussion groups.

LIVING FLAME PRESS

Box 74, Locust Valley, N.Y. 11560

QUANTITY

_____	Spiritual Direction — 4.95
_____	The Returning Sun — 2.50
_____	Living Here and Hereafter — 2.95
_____	Praying With Scripture in the Holy Land — 2.45
_____	Discernment — 3.50
_____	A Desert Place — 1.95
_____	Mourning: The Healing Journey — 2.50
_____	The Born-Again Catholic — 3.50
_____	Wisdom Instructs Her Children — 3.50
_____	Discovering Pathways to Prayer — 2.95
_____	Grains of Wheat — 2.50
_____	Bread for the Eating — 2.50
_____	Desert Silence — 2.50
_____	Who Is This God You Pray To — 2.50
_____	Union With the Lord in Prayer — 1.50
_____	Attaining Spiritual Maturity — 1.50
_____	Praying With Mary — 3.50
_____	Linger With Me — 3.50
_____	Book of Revelation — 2.50

NAME_____

ADDRESS _____

CITY_____ STATE_____ ZIP _____

Payment enclosed. Kindly include $.70 postage and handling on orders up to $5; $1.00 on orders up to $10; more than $10 but less than $50 add 10% of total; over $50 add 8% of total. Canadian residents add 20% exchange rate, plus postage and handling.

LIVING FLAME PRESS

Box 74, Locust Valley, N.Y. 11560

QUANTITY

_____	Spiritual Direction — 4.95
_____	The Returning Sun — 2.50
_____	Living Here and Hereafter — 2.95
_____	Praying With Scripture in the Holy Land — 2.45
_____	Discernment — 3.50
_____	A Desert Place — 1.95
_____	Mourning: The Healing Journey — 2.50
_____	The Born-Again Catholic — 3.50
_____	Wisdom Instructs Her Children — 3.50
_____	Discovering Pathways to Prayer — 2.95
_____	Grains of Wheat — 2.50
_____	Bread for the Eating — 2.50
_____	Desert Silence — 2.50
_____	Who Is This God You Pray To — 2.50
_____	Union With the Lord in Prayer — 1.50
_____	Attaining Spiritual Maturity — 1.50
_____	Praying With Mary — 3.50
_____	Linger With Me — 3.50
_____	Book of Revelation — 2.50

NAME _____

ADDRESS _____

CITY_____ STATE_____ ZIP _____

Payment enclosed. Kindly include $.70 postage and handling on orders up to $5; $1.00 on orders up to $10; more than $10 but less than $50 add 10% of total; over $50 add 8% of total. Canadian residents add 20% exchange rate, plus postage and handling.